The Medieval World

The Medieval World

Rebecca Stefoff

BENCHMARK BOOKS

MARSHALL CAVENDISH
NEW YORK

❄ ❄ ❄

Benchmark Books · Marshall Cavendish Corporation · 99 White Plains Road · Tarrytown, New York 10591-9001
www.marshallcavendish.us · Copyright © 2005 Rebecca Stefoff · All rights reserved. No part of this book may be reproduced or
utilized in any form or by any means electronic or mechanical including photocopying, recording, or by any information storage and
retrieval system, without permission from the copyright holders. · All Internet sites were available and accurate when sent to press.
Library of Congress Cataloging-in-Publication Data · Stefoff, Rebecca, 1951– · The medieval world / by Rebecca Stefoff. · p. cm. —
(World historical atlases) · Summary: Text plus historical and contemporary maps provide an overview of the history and culture of
Europe during the Middle Ages. Includes bibliographical references and index. · ISBN 0-7614-1642-0 · 1. Civilization, Medieval—
Juvenile literature. 2. Civilization, Medieval—Maps—Juvenile literature. 3. Middle Ages—Juvenile literature. 4. Europe—Social life and
customs—Juvenile literature. 5. Byzantine Empire—History—Juvenile literature. 6. Cities and towns, Medieval—Juvenile literature.
[1. Middle Ages. 2. Civilization, Medieval.] I. Title II. Series: Stefoff, Rebecca, 1951– . World historical atlases. · D117.S75 2003
909.07—dc22 · 2003022139 · Printed in China · 3 5 6 4 2 · Book design by Sonia Chaghatzbanian

Photo research by Linda Sykes Picture Research, Inc., Hilton Head, SC

The photographs in this book are used by permission and through the courtesy of: Biblioteca Nazionale Marciana, Venice/Dagli
Orti/The Art Archive: front cover; Dagli Orti/The Art Archive: back cover, 20-21; Adam Woolfitt/Corbis: ii-iii, 6-7; William
Manning/Corbis: 10; Patrick Durand/Corbis Sygma: 13; Musee de la Tapisserie Bayeux/Dagli Orti/The Art Archive: 14; Museum der
Stadt Wien/Dagli Orti/The Art Archive: 18; fresco, Vezzolano, Italy/The Art Archive: 19; Museo Naval, Madrid, Spain/Dagli Orti/The
Art Archive: 24; Musee Conde, Chantilly, France/Dagli Orti/The Art Archive: 27; Stapleton Collection/Corbis: 29; Topkapi Museum,
Istanbul, Turkey/Dagli Orti/The Art Archive: 31; Pinacoteca Nazionale di Siena/ Dagli Orti/The Art Archive: 32-33; Saint Sebastian
Chapel, Lanslevillard, Savoy/Dagli Orti/The Art Archive: 35; Eileen Tweedy/Bibliotheque Naitonale, Paris, France/The Art Archive: 36;
Biblioteca Estense, Modena/Dagli Orti/The Art Archive: 39; British Library/The Art Archive: 40.

Contents

CHAPTER ONE

The Rise of
the European States

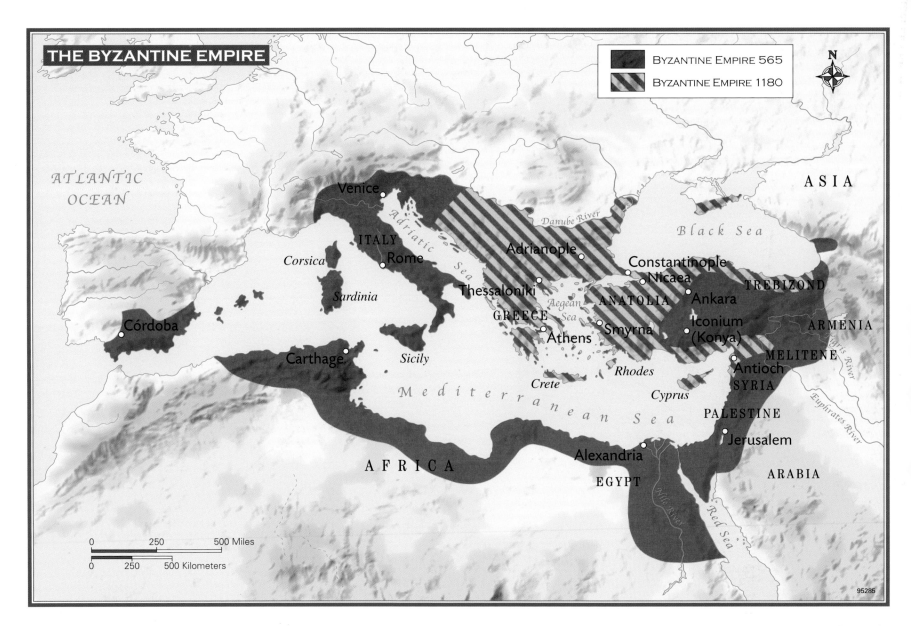

THE BYZANTINE EMPIRE

██	BYZANTINE EMPIRE 565
╱╱	BYZANTINE EMPIRE 1180

ATLANTIC OCEAN

Venice

ITALY

Córdoba

Corsica

Rome

Sardinia

Carthage

Sicily

AFRICA

Adriatic Sea

Danube River

Adrianople

Thessaloniki

GREECE

Aegean Sea

Athens

Smyrna

Crete

Rhodes

Mediterranean Sea

Black Sea

Constantinople

Nicaea

ANATOLIA

Ankara

Iconium (Konya)

Cyprus

TREBIZOND

ARMENIA

MELITENE

Antioch

SYRIA

PALESTINE

Jerusalem

Alexandria

EGYPT

Nile River

Red Sea

ASIA

Tigris River

Euphrates River

ARABIA

0   250   500 Miles

0   250   500 Kilometers

95285

For most of its existence, the Byzantine empire consisted of Anatolia, Greece, Syria, Palestine, and Egypt. In the sixth century Emperor Justinian I enlarged the empire to its greatest size by capturing territory that had belonged to the ancient Roman empire, including Italy and North Africa. But the Byzantine army and navy could not defend such a vast region. Invaders from Europe, Russia, Persia, and Arabia conquered parts of it until, by the twelfth century, the Byzantine empire was a fraction of its former size.

Europe's medieval period lasted roughly a thousand years. It is sometimes called the Middle Ages because it is sandwiched between the ancient era, which ended with the fall of the Roman **empire** around 500 C.E., and the modern era, which started with the rise of Renaissance culture around 1400 C.E. Medieval Europeans didn't think of themselves as living in the Middle Ages. That term came into use in the sixteenth century, when historians began dividing the past into periods. They saw that while each period of history had its own special features, each was also shaped by what had come before it. One important feature of the Middle Ages was the way the breakup of the old Roman empire gave birth to new states and new governments in Europe.

THE BYZANTINE EMPIRE AND THE WEST

In 395 C.E. the rulers of Rome split the empire into two parts. The western Roman empire was located entirely in Europe and ruled from the ancient capital city of Rome. The eastern Roman empire spread across Greece, Turkey, and the Near East. It was ruled from the rich and powerful city of Constantinople (today the Turkish city of Istanbul). Constantinople's old name was Byzantium, which is why the eastern Roman empire was often called the Byzantine empire.

Most Byzantines, like western Romans, were Christians. Also like the western Romans, the Byzantines saw themselves as the heirs of ancient Rome. Both realms were influenced by Roman culture, and both felt that their right to control territory stemmed from Rome's conquests. But the two empires faced different fates. The western Roman empire fell into chaos, taken over by German invaders from beyond its borders. The Byzantine empire remained unified under the rule of its emperors, but over time it lost territory to Persia (now Iran); to **nomadic** invaders from southeastern Russia; and to Turks, Mongols, and other warriors from central Asia.

Byzantium and western Europe were allies, but they were also rivals. As

The domes of the church of San Marco in Venice. For hundreds of years this Italian city was closely linked to Byzantium, sometimes in war, often in trade or alliance. Byzantine architects and artists helped create many of the city's landmarks, including San Marco. Domes like these are found on many churches and buildings in the Byzantine capital of Constantinople, now known as Istanbul.

Christian realms, the two stood united against non-Christian enemies, but they followed separate forms of Christianity, each claiming that its version was the true one. The Roman Catholic church of western Europe and the Eastern Orthodox church of Byzantium competed to convert non-Christians to their faiths. The two empires differed in other ways as well. The Roman language, Latin, remained the language of learning and religion in the west, while Greek became the official language of the Byzantine empire.

The two realms came into open conflict in the tenth century when Norman warriors, originally from western France, attacked Byzantine territory in Greece. The Byzantine emperor Alexios II managed to drive the invaders out of Greece. He then built new ties with the West by establishing trade relations between the Byzantine empire and the Italian city of Venice. This partnership gave Byzantium the support of Venice's powerful navy against enemies that attacked Byzantine lands by sea—even against other western

European powers. In return, Venice made huge profits from trading in silk, spices, and other Asian goods that passed through Constantinople. For the rest of the Middle Ages, Byzantium and the West remained linked by ties of trade and business, in spite of political conflicts that arose from time to time.

THE FRANKS

France was known to the ancient Romans as Gaul and was a **province** of their empire. In the fifth century, as the western Roman empire was falling apart, a Germanic people called the Franks invaded Gaul. A leader named Clovis united the Frankish tribes before 500 C.E., founding a **dynasty** that ruled France until the eighth century. Later another royal family gained power and produced Charlemagne, one of the most influential rulers of the early Middle Ages. Charlemagne, who came to the throne in 768, was more than the king of France. He conquered an empire that reached into what is now Germany, established a strong and well-organized central government, and built a royal school and library to promote learning and the arts.

After Charlemagne's death in 814, his descendants divided his empire. The region that is now France was gradually chipped away into many small realms ruled by princes, dukes, and counts. A king still sat on the throne of France, but he had little more power than his nobles. However, things began to change during the reign of Hugh Capet, who was king from 987 to 996. The ruling family he founded, the Capetian dynasty, governed France for most of the rest of the medieval period and eventually regained the power and authority that the **monarchy** had lost after Charlemagne's time. In the twelfth century, the Capetian kings shrewdly granted new privileges—such as the right to gather taxes and administer justice—to bishops, town leaders, and the officials who oversaw the management of the royal households. As a result, these groups became loyal to the monarchy. At the same time, Capetian kings made war on some of the lesser nobles and seized their lands. As the kings' power and territory grew, the greater nobles began bowing to royal authority. By the fourteenth century, the might of the nobles had been greatly reduced, and the monarchy's authority was firmly established across France, one of the most cultured, prosperous, and politically powerful nations in Europe.

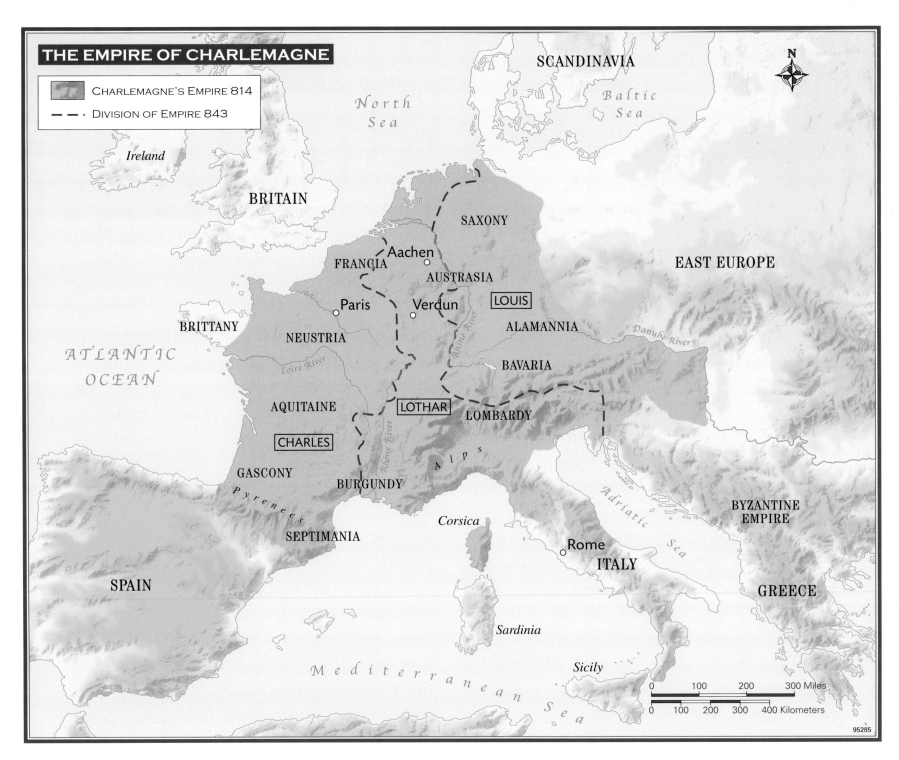

THE EMPIRE OF CHARLEMAGNE

Charlemagne's Empire 814

Division of Empire 843

SCANDINAVIA

North Sea

Baltic Sea

Ireland

BRITAIN

EAST EUROPE

SAXONY

Aachen

FRANCIA

AUSTRASIA

LOUIS

Paris

Verdun

ALAMANNIA

Danube River

BRITTANY

ATLANTIC OCEAN

NEUSTRIA

Rhine River

Loire River

BAVARIA

AQUITAINE

LOTHAR

LOMBARDY

CHARLES

Rhône River

Alps

GASCONY

BURGUNDY

Adriatic Sea

BYZANTINE EMPIRE

Pyrenees

Corsica

SEPTIMANIA

Rome

ITALY

GREECE

SPAIN

Sardinia

Sicily

Mediterranean Sea

| 0 | 100 | 200 | 300 Miles |
| 0 | 100 | 200 | 300 | 400 Kilometers |

95285

With the force of his powerful personality, his strong army, and the support of loyal nobles, Charlemagne ruled an empire that covered much of Europe. After Charlemagne's death in 814, his son ruled as Louis I, but Louis was less effective as emperor than his mighty father. In 843 the Treaty of Verdun divided the empire between three of Louis I's sons—Charles, Lothar, and Louis.

The last Capetian king, Charles IV, died in 1328 without producing a son to inherit the throne, so the French nobles chose one of his cousins as their new king. But the English felt that the French throne should rightfully have gone to their king, Edward III, Charles's nephew. The dispute over the French throne produced increasing tension until war broke out between the two countries in 1337. This long series of conflicts and invasions, known as the Hundred Years' War, ended in the middle of the fifteenth century.

ENGLAND

Like Gaul, the Roman province of England was invaded by Germanic peoples in the fifth century C.E. These invaders, the Angles and the Saxons, established eight small kingdoms in what is now England. For years the Anglo-Saxon kingdoms fought among themselves. By the early ninth century, however, the kingdom of Wessex had become more powerful than the others. King Egbert of Wessex was ready to conquer some of his neighbors when a new threat appeared, forcing the Anglo-Saxons to unite against a common enemy—Viking invaders from Norway and Denmark. A

The Hundred Years' War produced an unlikely heroine: a French peasant girl named Joan of Arc, who claimed that God was guiding her to attack an English army that was besieging the city of Orléans. The French gave her command of the army, and she drove the English from the area. The king and people of France idolized Joan, but a year later she was captured by the English. They convicted her of religious crimes and burned her at the stake.

Viking army overran most of England, but Egbert's heir, Alfred, kept Wessex from falling to the invaders. Alfred then forged an **alliance** between Wessex and the Anglo-Saxon kingdom of Mercia to fight the Vikings. The English finally succeeded in driving out the Vikings in the

The Bayeaux Tapestry, made in France around 1100, is a band of linen embroidered with seventy-two scenes showing the history of the Norman conquest of England. In this scene, Saxon warriors under King Harold II hurl spears at the invading Normans at the Battle of Hastings—a conflict the Saxons lost.

eleventh century.

But the Vikings *did* conquer England—in a way. In 1066 an army of Normans, led by a warrior called William the Conqueror, invaded England. They came from Normandy in western France, but many historians believe they were descended from Vikings who had settled on the French coast. For the rest of the Middle Ages, England was ruled by Norman kings and then by the Angevin dynasty, founded in 1154 by King Henry II, a great-grandson of William the Conqueror. Some Norman and Angevin kings also held territory in France. While these kings sat on the English throne, England was closely

14

connected with affairs on the European continent. At other times, however, the English saw themselves as culturally and politically separate from the rest of Europe. France and England often regarded each other as rivals, if not outright enemies.

GERMANY

Early in the Middle Ages, Charlemagne's empire included much of what is now Germany. When the empire was divided after Charlemagne's death, the emperor's son Louis received Germany—a forested, frontier region occupied by tribes with a strong tradition of governing themselves. As in France, local leaders ruled their own territories and resisted the king's efforts to control them. Over time, as tribal leaders took more formal titles, Germany became a patchwork of small princedoms and dukedoms. The German monarchy continued to exist, but the king—who was elected by the nobles—had little real power or authority. Then, in 936, a Saxon duke named Otto became king of Germany. Skilled and ambitious, Otto strengthened royal authority and enlarged his territory by conquering the dukedom of Franconia and many other small German realms.

Sharing Power with Parliament

Medieval kings' powers were great—but not unlimited. In England in 1215, rebellious nobles and church officials forced King John to sign the Magna Carta, a document that reduced the monarch's power and stated that even kings had to obey the law. Although John and later kings sometimes ignored the Magna Carta, the document was a legal basis for limiting the taxes that kings could demand from the people and even for removing unpopular kings from power. Later in the medieval period, the assembly known as parliament gained greater power in England. Made up of nobles, church officials, and representatives of the nation's towns and counties, parliament became the voice of the country. As time went on, the English monarchs found it more and more difficult—even impossible—to wage war, raise taxes, or change existing laws without the consent of parliament.

GERMANY

North Sea

DENMARK

Baltic Sea

Lübeck

Hamburg

Bremen

FRIESLAND

EASTPHALIA

POLAND

Utrecht

SAXONY

Brandenburg

Magdeburg

Weser River

Elbe River

Odra River

Antwerp

WESTPHALIA

LOWER LORRAINE

Cologne

HESSE

THURINGIA

FLANDERS

BRABANT

FRANCONIA

Frankfurt

Prague

BOHEMIA

Rhine River

Moselle River

Mainz

Trier

Worms

Nuremberg

Regensberg

MORAVIA

Metz

UPPER LORRAINE

Strasbourg

BAVARIA

AUSTRIA

Vienna

Danube River

FRANCE

ALSACE

Augsburg

Salzburg

SWABIA

Lech River

Danube River

CARINTHIA

HUNGARY

Geneva

VERONA

BURGUNDY

Legnano

Milan

Verona

Turin

LOMBARDY

Venice

Rhone River

Po River

Genoa

ITALY

Adriatic Sea

PROVENCE

Pisa

Mediterranean Sea

Legend:
- GERMAN EMPIRE 962
- OTTO I'S INFLUENCE
- OTTO I'S CONQUESTS

Scale: 0   50   100 Miles
0   50   100   150 Kilometers

95285

In addition to conquering some of Germany's neighbors—such as Austria—Otto I also extended German influence by treaty or by the threat of war. Under his rule, Germany controlled most of central Europe and northern Italy. For hundreds of years after his reign, Germany would swing back and forth between unifying into an empire and breaking apart into several small independent states.

In the twelfth century, a dynasty called the Hohenstaufens came to power. Under a series of powerful kings, the Hohenstaufens gained control of Sicily, parts of northern Italy and Poland, and the coasts of the North and Baltic seas. Germany changed greatly during their rule. Huge areas of forest were cleared and turned into productive farms. Towns and cities grew, cathedrals and schools appeared, and culture and trade thrived.

The Hohenstaufen dynasty ended in 1250 with the death of its last strong king, Frederick II. For a few decades Germany was torn by power struggles among a dozen or more princes. Then two dynasties, the Luxembourgs and the Habsburgs, began competing for the throne. First the Habsburgs held power, then the Luxembourgs. In the mid-fifteenth century, as the Middle Ages drew to a close, the Habsburgs again took control. By this time, however, the monarchy had lost much of its power. For several centuries the German kings' authority had declined as the power of nobles, church officials, city leaders, and wealthy merchants grew. By the fifteenth century, the monarchy had less power than the realm's officials and rural nobles.

THE PAPACY

During the Middle Ages, the pope, the head of the Roman Catholic church, became not just a major religious leader but a political leader as well. The pope's office and authority, called the papacy, enjoyed varying degrees of power through the centuries.

The main officials of the early church were the bishops, each of whom guided his own community of Christians. Gradually the bishop of Rome came to be seen as the most important of these figures. Even before the end of the western Roman empire, the emperors had granted the bishops of Rome authority over all other bishops. By 1000 the bishop of Rome was known as the pope. Elected by high church officials called cardinals, the pope was the supreme leader of the Roman Catholic church.

Early in the medieval period, the papacy gained influence under Gregory I, who became pope in 590. In addition to being a religious leader, Gregory was involved in political and military affairs, such as organizing the defense of Rome against Germanic invaders. Papal power and influence grew through the following centuries, when rulers such as Charlemagne gave large

What's in a Name?

The kings of medieval Germany wanted to be seen as Charlemagne's heirs, as great and as powerful as he had been. So they adopted his title of emperor. Charlemagne, in his own time, had taken the title to link himself to the rulers of ancient Rome—in 800 C.E. he had Pope Leo III crown him emperor of the Romans. In 962 Pope John XII gave King Otto I of Germany the same title, and by the eleventh century the German kings were calling their realm the Roman empire. In 1155 Frederick I Barbarossa of the Hohenstaufen dynasty started calling it the Holy Empire to suggest that God supported his reign. The term *Holy Roman Empire* came into use in 1254 for the ever-changing collection of states— usually including Austria and often parts of Italy and France—that the German kings ruled. The title Holy Roman emperor lasted for centuries, although it started to lose its importance as the modern nation-states of Europe acquired political power and identities of their own. Fifty years before the last Holy Roman emperor, Francis II, gave up the title in 1806, the French writer Voltaire scornfully wrote that "This agglomeration [grouping] which was called and still calls itself the Holy Roman Empire is neither holy, nor Roman, nor an empire."

A window in the cathedral of Saint Stephen in Vienna, Austria, depicts Frederick I, who became king of Germany in 1152. Three years later the pope crowned him Holy Roman emperor. Frederick spent most of his reign leading military campaigns into Italy, but in spite of some successes he failed to conquer the peninsula. He died in 1190, drowned while crossing a river in Turkey on his way to fight in the Third Crusade.

Gregory I, pope from 590 to 604, was one of the most influential popes of the Middle Ages. He held political power equal to that of most kings, organized a system for managing the church's enormous holdings of land and money, and wrote hundreds of letters and dozens of books on religious subjects. Known as Pope Gregory the Great, he is a saint of the Roman Catholic church.

pieces of land to the popes. During the tenth century, however, without strong central rulers in France and Germany to support the popes, papal power declined. Italian nobles fought over the papacy, and many popes were controlled by powerful families. For example, Pope John XI (931–935), the son of an Italian noblewoman from the city of Ravenna, followed her orders.

Beginning in the eleventh century, the papacy took a new direction and focused on religious concerns such as reforming corrupt church practices. Popes pitted themselves against powerful rulers by insisting that only popes, not kings, could appoint bishops. Innocent III, pope from 1198 to 1216, claimed broad powers for the papacy and tried to act on those claims. He also meddled in the politics of England, Italy, France, and the Holy Roman Empire. The ambitions of Innocent and some of the popes who followed him created tension and power struggles between the Catholic church and the monarchies of the later Middle Ages. In one such power struggle, the Holy Roman Empire went to war with the papacy over territory in Italy. The kings of France, competing for the popes' favor, moved the headquarters of the papacy to France for most of the fourteenth century in order to gain more influence over the popes. These conflicts drove the papacy into disorder. At times, two or even three rival popes claimed power, and the authority and influence of the papacy again declined in the late Middle Ages.

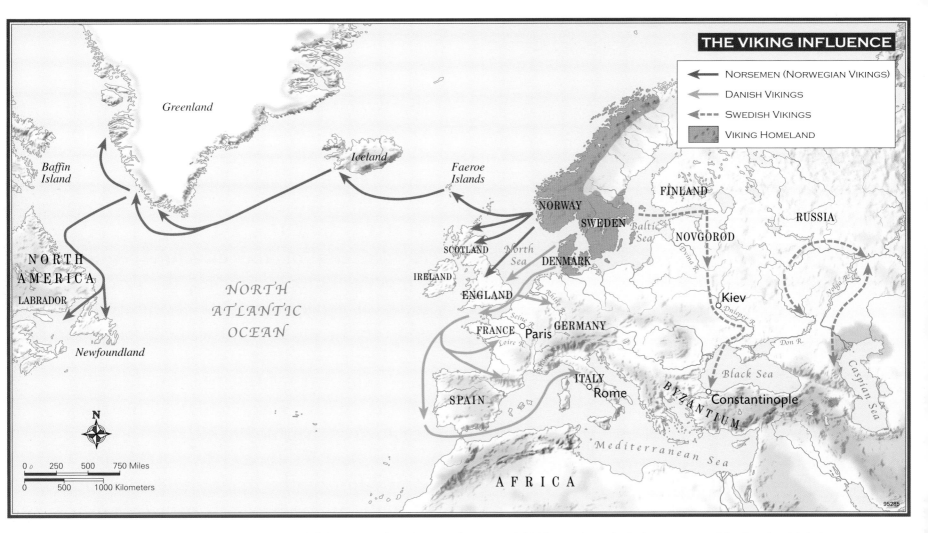

Legend:
- ← NORSEMEN (NORWEGIAN VIKINGS)
- ← DANISH VIKINGS
- ←--- SWEDISH VIKINGS
- ▨ VIKING HOMELAND

The Vikings' North Atlantic voyages left legacies for the modern world. Vikings founded the nation of Iceland, which is still inhabited mostly by their descendants. Viking settlements in Greenland gave Denmark a claim to that enormous island, which it still owns. But other Viking travels were far more significant, shaping the culture and history of lands from England to Russia.

tribes (the word *slave* comes from Slav). In the tenth century, Viking adventurers founded a settlement where the city of Novgorod now stands. This city-state grew and prospered and became known as Rus, from the Arabic and Slavic word for Viking. It was the beginning of modern Russia. As Rus expanded in the following two centuries, the culture of its Scandinavian rulers blended with that of the Slavic people they ruled.

Vikings also ventured into the Byzantine empire. Viking raiders tried at least once—without success—to capture Constantinople. A different group of Vikings was already established within the city, however. They were **mercenary** troops called Varangians, hired to protect

Money Crosses Miles

Money changed hands often in parts of medieval Europe. Coins found in Scandinavia are evidence of links between northern Europe and the Islamic world several thousand miles away. More than 80,000 silver dirhams, coins of the Islamic empire, have been found in Sweden alone, while Denmark and Norway have yielded smaller numbers. Made between the late eighth and early eleventh centuries, the dirhams probably reached Scandinavia through trade, as payment to the Varangians and other Viking mercenaries, and as loot or **tribute** from Slavic regions that used Islamic money. Most Islamic coins found in Scandinavia were in hoards, collections of wealth buried for safekeeping. Some hoards also contained silver jewelry, probably made from melted-down dirhams. Not all of the Muslim money in Scandinavia was hidden away, however. Islamic silver paid for shipbuilding, land, and other parts of the growing economies of both Russia and Scandinavia during the tenth and eleventh centuries, the height of the Viking Age.

the Byzantine emperors. The Varangian Guard remained an elite force in Constantinople until the city fell at the end of the medieval period.

THE CRUSADES

At the end of the eleventh century, Christian Europe launched the first in a series of expeditions that continued, on and off, for the rest of the medieval period. These were the Crusades, and they were intended to drive the Muslims out of the Near East, which Christians regarded as their holy land.

The First Crusade (1095–1099) was a joint effort by the Byzantine empire and western European powers such as France. The warriors of this Crusade recaptured some Anatolian cities for the Byzantines and also freed Antioch and Jerusalem from the Muslims. Some of the First Crusade's leaders founded small Christian city-states, called the crusader kingdoms, in the Holy Land. These endured for several centuries. Future Crusades came to the aid of these kingdoms, which Muslim armies tried often to recapture.

Crusades occurred throughout the Middle Ages, but none was as successful as the First Crusade. Some were complete failures. The knights of the Second

A fifteenth-century illustration shows the forces of the First Crusade capturing the ancient city of Antioch in what is now Turkey. The success of the First Crusade made Europeans believe that they would soon drive the Muslims out of the Middle East. They were wrong.

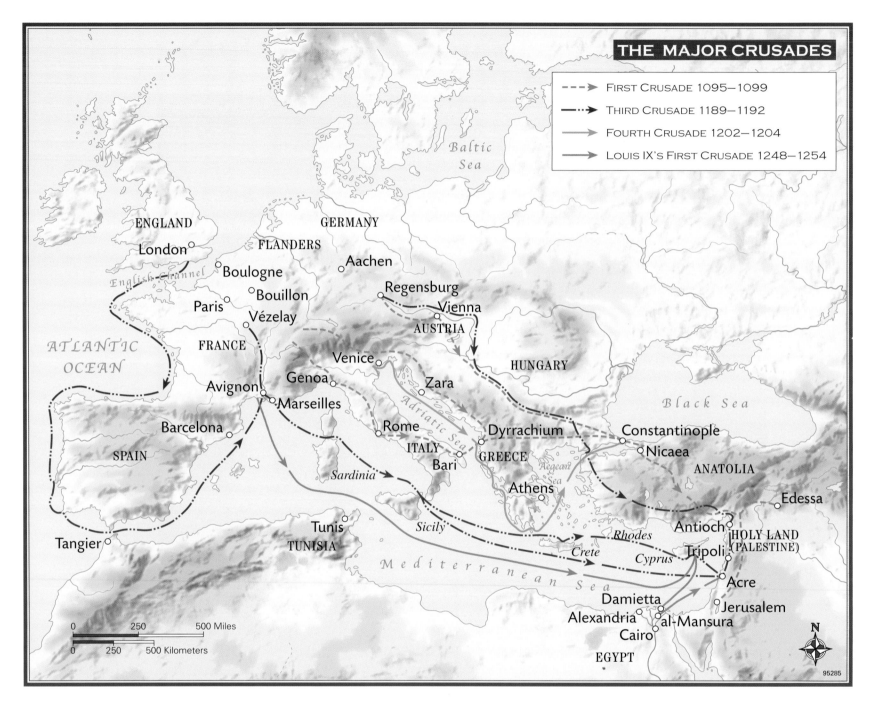

THE MAJOR CRUSADES

- - - ▸ FIRST CRUSADE 1095–1099
— ·— ▸ THIRD CRUSADE 1189–1192
————▸ FOURTH CRUSADE 1202–1204
————▸ LOUIS IX'S FIRST CRUSADE 1248–1254

ENGLAND
London
FLANDERS
Boulogne
Bouillon
Paris
Vézelay
GERMANY
Aachen
Regensburg
Vienna
AUSTRIA
HUNGARY
English Channel
ATLANTIC OCEAN
FRANCE
Avignon
Genoa
Marseilles
Venice
Zara
Adriatic Sea
Dyrrachium
Constantinople
Nicaea
Black Sea
Barcelona
SPAIN
Rome
ITALY
Bari
GREECE
Athens
Aegean Sea
ANATOLIA
Edessa
Sardinia
Tangier
Tunis
TUNISIA
Sicily
Mediterranean Sea
Crete
Rhodes
Cyprus
Antioch
HOLY LAND (PALESTINE)
Tripoli
Acre
Jerusalem
Damietta
Alexandria
al-Mansura
Cairo
EGYPT

0 250 500 Miles
0 250 500 Kilometers

N

95285

The First Crusade established a few small Christian states in the Near East. After the Muslim leader Saladdin recaptured Jerusalem in 1187, the Third Crusade was launched to get it back. The attempt was only partly successful—the Crusaders won the port of Acre, but not Jerusalem. The Fourth Crusade ended in disorder when the Crusaders attacked and looted Constantinople, making it bitterly hostile to Europeans. In the Seventh Crusade, Louis IX of France tried to regain Jerusalem by pitting Islamic leaders against each other, but failed. The Crusades never achieved the goal of "liberating" the Holy Land from the Muslims. But they did increase communication and trade between the Christian and Muslim worlds.

Crusade (1147–1149) ended up as Muslim slaves. The costly Fifth Crusade (1217–1221) failed to achieve its goal of capturing Egypt. The crusaders of King Louis IX of France (1248–1254) also failed to capture Egypt. During their attempt, the king fell into Muslim hands and had to pay a high ransom for his freedom. In 1291 the Muslims recaptured the last of the crusader kingdoms, taking complete control of the Near East. Later crusaders achieved a few minor victories, such as a successful raid on the Egyptian port of Alexandria in 1300, but they never seriously challenged Muslim dominance in the Holy Land.

Although the Crusades failed to liberate the Near East from Muslim rule, they introduced western Europe to Islamic culture and learning. They also increased trade between the two worlds. Venice, Pisa, and Genoa—Italian cities with large trading fleets—benefited greatly not only from this growth in trade but from the Crusades themselves, which often required the use of their ships for transportation.

THE MONGOLS IN RUSSIA

The Mongols were nomadic herders living in Mongolia in northeastern Asia. At the

For Europeans of the late Middle Ages, Genghis Khan's Mongol empire was a mysterious and possibly friendly power in the distant East. European rulers tried several times to woo the Mongols into joining them in an alliance against the Islamic empire of the Near East.

dawn of the thirteenth century, a leader known as Genghis Khan united the Mongol clans under his rule and set about building an empire. The well-organized Mongol army, famous for its horsemanship, seized control of northern China. Genghis next attacked and subdued Khwarizm, a strong Muslim kingdom in the central Asian regions now known as Tajikistan and Uzbekistan. He then conquered Afghanistan, northern Iran and Iraq, and southern Russia.

When Genghis Khan died in 1227, his three sons and one grandson divided up his empire. One son, Ögödei, expanded his territory in Russia and invaded eastern Europe. His armies reached the Danube River and had advanced to the gates of Vienna, Austria, when he died in 1241. Ögödei's death threw the Mongol empire into disorder, probably sparing Europe from a full-scale Mongol invasion. One part of Europe, however, remained under Mongol rule. Genghis's grandson Batu established a branch of the Mongol empire in Russia. Called the Golden Horde because of the gold roof on the dwelling of its khan, or ruler, this Mongol power had its capital at Saray, a city on the Volga River. Because of Islamic influence in the region, many of the khans who ruled after Batu were Muslims. They encouraged the mixing of the Mongols with Islamic central Asian Turks, and this blending produced an Islamic people known as the Tatars. The Golden Horde controlled an empire of Tatars in the south and Russians and Lithuanians in the north. By the end of the Middle Ages, however, fighting among Tatar princes and rebellions led by the Russians had torn apart the horde and destroyed Saray, the last European outpost of the once-great Mongol empire.

THE TURKS AND CONSTANTINOPLE

In the early Middle Ages, central Asia was the home of nomadic Turkish-speaking peoples. During the eighth century, most of these Turkish groups became Muslims. Later, some of them united under warlords to form armies of conquest. These warlords wanted to build empires, and all of them dreamed of capturing Constantinople.

In the eleventh century a group called the Seljuq Turks won control of much of the eastern Islamic world. They conquered Syria and, in 1071, beat a Byzantine army in the Battle of Manzikert. After their victory,

A painting from 1520 shows the Ottoman sultan, or ruler. Less than seventy years earlier, Ottoman armies had conquered Constantinople, marking the end of the Byzantine empire and bringing Greece and other parts of eastern Europe, as well as all of Turkey, under Islamic rule.

the Seljuqs easily took large areas of Anatolia from the Byzantines. Mongols later overthrew the Seljuq rulers in Anatolia and seized their lands. The Mongols in turn were overthrown by yet another Turkish people, the Ottomans, who rose to power in eastern Turkey. During the fourteenth century, the Ottomans seized several key cities and ports from the Byzantine empire, reducing the Anatolian holdings of the once-mighty empire to Constantinople and a few nearby coastal settlements. The Ottomans also pushed into Byzantine territory in eastern Europe. Their armies swept into Bulgaria, Serbia, and other lands in the mountainous Balkan Peninsula north of Greece. Next they set their sights on the crown jewel, Constantinople. They laid siege to the city in 1453. Although the Byzantine capital had held off many attackers in its long history, the Ottomans greatly outnumbered its defenders. After a few months, Constantinople fell to the Turks, and the Byzantine empire came to an end.

CHAPTER THREE
The Late Middle Ages

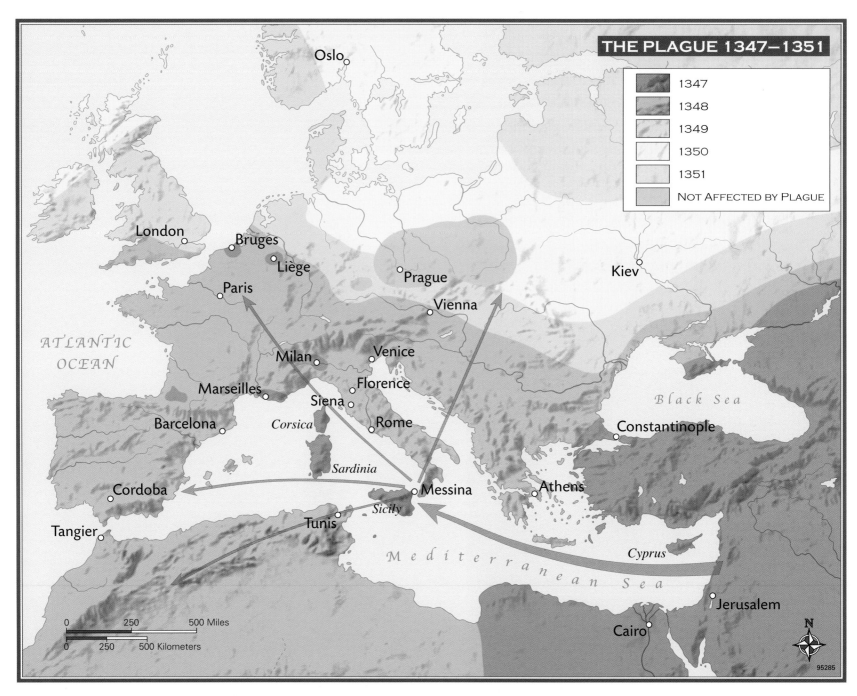

THE PLAGUE 1347–1351

■	1347
■	1348
■	1349
□	1350
■	1351
■	Not Affected by Plague

Oslo

London

Bruges

Liège

Paris

Prague

Vienna

Kiev

ATLANTIC
OCEAN

Milan

Venice

Florence

Marseilles

Siena

Rome

Black Sea

Barcelona

Corsica

Constantinople

Cordoba

Sardinia

Messina

Athens

Tangier

Tunis

Sicily

Cyprus

Mediterranean Sea

Jerusalem

Cairo

N

0   250   500 Miles

0   250   500 Kilometers

95285

Historians believe that the plague reached Europe on ships from Asia that landed at the Sicilian port of Messina. From there the disease spread rapidly across Europe in a large-scale epidemic called the Black Death. Epidemiologists—scientists who study how disease is spread—do not know why a few areas in Europe remained free of the plague.

Wars, invasions, and alliances shaped the political history of the medieval world and redrew its maps. But other changes took place as well, social shifts that affected the lives of countless individuals. During the first half of the medieval period, most of Europe was organized into **feudal** agricultural societies. **Peasant** farmers answered to landowners, landowners to higher-ranking nobles, and higher-ranking nobles to kings. The feudal system broke down in the second half of the medieval period as merchants and townspeople grew more numerous and gained greater economic power. The late Middle Ages was a time of upheaval, unrest, and social change, but it was also a time of increased independence and wider economic and educational opportunities.

THE BLACK DEATH

The Black Death was a natural disaster that first struck Europe in 1347, killing 25 to 45 percent of the continent's population within five years. It was an epidemic of the disease called the plague, which dramatically changed the society and economy of the later medieval world.

The epidemic began in Asia and spread to Europe on Italian merchant ships. In 1347 Europe's first cases of plague appeared in the Sicilian port of Messina. The disease soon swept through mainland Italy, killing half the population of Venice, and then on to France, the Netherlands, England, Germany, Scandinavia, and Russia. Plague took two forms, pneumonic and bubonic, both deadly. Bubonic plague, in which victims develop large blackish swellings called buboes, gave

Some doctors tried to treat the plague by cutting open the swellings called buboes. Others simply shut sufferers up in their houses to keep the disease from spreading. None of their treatments was effective. Many Europeans believed that the plague had supernatural causes. This fifteenth-century illustration of a doctor treating plague victims also shows a devil and an angel who seem to be determining the sick person's fate.

Royal troops massacre the rebellious French peasants of the Jacquerie. By hinting that the social order could be overturned, peasant uprisings terrified Europe's kings and nobles, who ruthlessly crushed any sign of revolt.

the disease the name by which most Europeans knew it: the Black Death.

The plague's effects were severe and long lasting. So many people died that whole urban neighborhoods and large stretches of countryside were left nearly empty. Production of food and goods fell sharply due to the lack of labor. One positive result of the tragedy, though, was that farmers and craftspeople became highly valued in the years after the Black Death. Many saw improvements in their wages and standards of living. The Black Death had cultural effects as well. It shook people's confidence in religion and learning because neither priests nor doctors could save plague victims once they were infected. Some felt that the disease was God's punishment for their sins, while others blamed it on groups they feared, such as the Jews. By killing kings, popes, and peasants alike, the Black Death made many medieval Europeans feel that the social order binding them was fragile. To make matters worse, the plague returned at least once every generation for the next several centuries.

PEASANT UPRISINGS

Medieval peasants worked hard, lived mostly in poverty, and paid taxes in the form of labor, crops, or money. The harsh conditions of their lives and ever-growing taxes sparked occasional peasant rebellions across Europe, from Spain to Hungary. Two of the biggest peasant uprisings took place in France and England, probably triggered by the Hundred Years' War and the Black Death. Kings had taxed their citizens heavily to pay for the war, while the Black Death had disturbed the social order and led ordinary people to question the power of the nobility, who could do nothing to stop the plague.

The French uprising, called the Jacquerie, occurred in 1358 around Paris. It involved not just rural peasants but also craftspeople, village priests, and others who resented the unchecked power of the noble class. The rebels were violent, slaughtering not just noblemen but women and children as well. Royal forces responded swiftly and harshly, luring Guillaume Cale, the leader of the Jacquerie, into a trap. They then crushed all signs of revolt, killing the peasants who had rebelled and even some who had not.

The English peasants' uprising began in 1381 with an attack on royal tax officials in the county of Essex. It soon spread to half a dozen other counties. Led by a

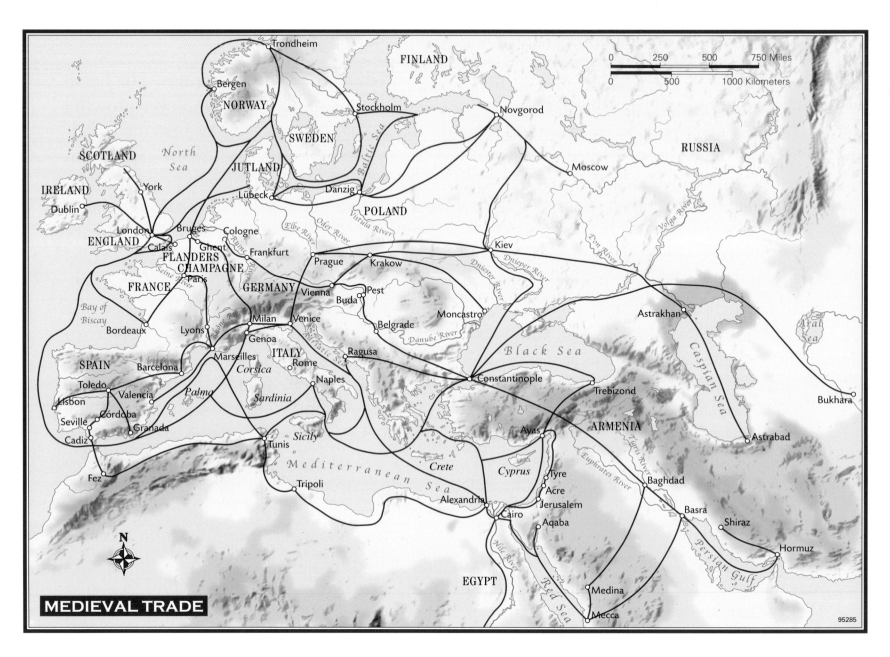

MEDIEVAL TRADE

Most of the major medieval trade routes involved water. They crossed seas, followed rivers, or ran along coastlines. In spite of such dangers as storms and pirates, travel by water was generally safer than travel by land, and it was almost always faster. Still, a network of roads knitted together cities and towns. Carried on the backs of pack animals or in wagons, goods as varied as English wool, Spanish olive oil, and Swedish dried fish crossed Europe. So did more exotic goods, such as silks and spices from China and India, which reached Europe by way of Constantinople, Cairo, Baghdad, and other eastern trading centers.

peasant named Wat Tyler, a rebel band marched to London and destroyed a palace. Tyler then forced King Richard II to meet with him and other rebels. But the peasant leader was killed in a fight with the king's soldiers, and Richard slyly convinced the other rebels to leave London. Royal forces managed to end the English rebellion less violently than in France.

MERCHANTS AND TRADE

Long-distance trade, a feature of the Roman empire, all but disappeared once the empire fell. As a result, communities and regions became more isolated from one another and more self-supporting. After the tenth century, however, trade thrived again. Northern European traders traveled the North Sea, the Baltic Sea, and the rivers that flowed into them. This region exported timber, wool, and grain and imported wine and large quantities of salt for preserving dried fish.

The growth of cities in the late Middle Ages gave rise to works of literature and art that compared and contrasted urban and rural life. This Italian artwork shows a gathering in a square, as laborers work in fields outside the city. Such images reflected the notion that there was a proper, orderly way of life for each setting. Those who broke the rules might end up like the three hanged men—a powerful warning to potential lawbreakers.

Medieval Travel

One of the milestones of medieval literature is *The Canterbury Tales,* written by Geoffrey Chaucer of England in the late fourteenth century. It is a collection of stories told by travelers making a religious pilgrimage. Like most medieval travelers, Chaucer's pilgrims—illustrated here in an image from the mid-fifteenth century—sought safety in numbers.

One strength of the Roman empire was its far-reaching network of good, stone-paved roads. During the Middle Ages, many of those roads fell into disrepair. Still, the basic routes remained—for those able and willing to risk travel. During the early Middle Ages, travel was rare and dangerous. Peasants were not allowed to leave their lord's property. People who could travel usually did so in large groups to protect themselves from bandits and kidnappers. Some went on official business—kings, popes, and their representatives regularly moved through their realms. Others made religious pilgrimages, visiting shrines in Rome or even far-off Jerusalem. Musicians and other performers also wandered from place to place to entertain courts and crowds—and they did so in safety because, by tradition, bandits gave safe passage to performers. Later in the Middle Ages, travel and transportation increased as the volume of trade grew. Travelers used waterways when they could, but to encourage trade and economic growth many communities decided to repair roads and build new bridges.

The North Sea ports of Brugge and Ghent were famed as centers of the cloth trade, while the trading ports of the Baltic Sea formed their own economic alliance, the Hanseatic League. Founded in the mid-fourteenth century, the league regulated commerce in regional products such as honey, wax, timber, and pitch (a natural tar used to seal the hulls of ships). Trade in southern Europe centered mostly on the Mediterranean Sea and included wine, olive oil, and grain. The most valuable goods in the southern trade, however, were luxury items from Asia and the Near East, including gems, silks, and spices.

Merchants bought and sold goods at fairs that took place in certain cities every year. These fairs attracted business from all over Europe. They had not only great economic importance but social significance as well. One of the biggest fairs was held in Champagne, France, from the twelfth century to the fourteenth. It and other fairs helped promote long-distance trade, which placed new power in the hands of the commercial segments of society: merchants; wagoners, shipowners, and other traders and transporters; craftspeople and tradespeople; and bankers. During the fourteenth century, however,

the Black Death and the Hundred Years' War brought a temporary decline in trade across most of western Europe.

THE GROWTH OF CITIES

The wars and invasions that ended the western Roman empire caused a decline in urban populations at the dawn of the Middle Ages. Some towns and cities were destroyed or completely abandoned. The early medieval world was largely rural and agricultural—industry and trade were much less important than producing food. The cities and towns that did remain were dominated by churches and often controlled by bishops. By the twelfth century, though, a more dynamic urban culture was flowering in western Europe.

Increased agricultural production led to food surpluses, which allowed some regions to expand beyond farming to pursue other industries, such as cloth making. Trade increased as towns and cities became centers of production and business. A new class of urban workers arose. It included craftspeople who sold goods and servants and laborers who sold their skills. Merchants, **guild** members, bankers, civic officials, and universities began to divide and share

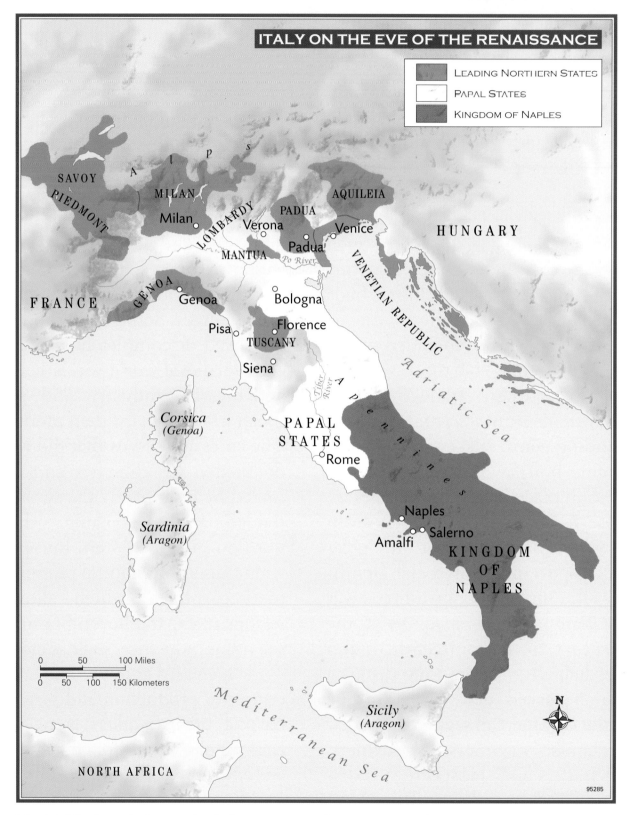

ITALY ON THE EVE OF THE RENAISSANCE

LEADING NORTHERN STATES
PAPAL STATES
KINGDOM OF NAPLES

By the end of the Middle Ages, Italy was divided among several major powers. The Kingdom of Naples ruled the south, the Papal States controlled the lands around the cities of Rome and Bologna, and a variety of strong, independent city-states existed in the north. The Renaissance sprouted in the northern Italian cities when scholars and artists began studying the heritage of ancient Greece and Rome. From there the Renaissance spread throughout Italy and to the rest of Europe, bringing new artistic styles, attitudes, and social orders.

local power, which no longer rested entirely with the church. Some towns became communes, self-governing communities. By the beginning of the fourteenth century, Europe had several metropolises. Its largest city was Paris, France, with a population perhaps as large as 200,000. The leading Italian cities—Florence, Venice, and Milan—had 100,000 people each.

A New Beginning

At the end of the Middle Ages came the Black Death, the Hundred Years' War, peasant rebellions, civil war in England (as various dynasties fought for the throne), and a general decline in trade and urban growth in western Europe. The late medieval period was bleak, yet two important processes were setting the stage for a new phase of history. One of these processes was scholarly; the other was geographic.

European scholars were rediscovering the ancient world. New translations and editions of Greek and Roman writings— many obtained from libraries and scholars in the Byzantine and Islamic worlds— reached universities and towns from Hungary to England. These works roused interest in ancient culture, art, philosophy, and history, and they inspired European writers and artists. At the same time, geographic knowledge increased. The Crusades had given Europeans a better understanding of the world beyond their borders. As the Middle Ages ended, Portuguese, English, and Spanish navigators began probing the Atlantic Ocean in search of new trade routes to Asia. By the time Christopher Columbus made his first voyage to the Americas in 1492–1493, the medieval period had come to a close, and Europeans entered a larger realm—the world of the **Renaissance**.

Glossary

alliance—An agreement among states to cooperate in defense, trade, or other activities.

dynasty—A series of rulers from the same family or group.

empire—A large political organization that contains more than one ethnic or language group; usually created by force.

feudal—Relating to a social and political organization based on lordship, in which lords held the land and people of lower rank owed them loyalty and service in exchange for protection.

guild—An association of professional or craft workers that set standards and prices for the services and goods produced by its members.

mercenary—A soldier for hire.

monarchy—Rule by kings.

nomadic—Relating to nomads, people who move from place to place rather than live in permanent settlements.

pagan—Related to ancient or primitive religions; medieval Europeans viewed all non-Christians as pagans.

peasant—A rural agricultural worker, generally someone who lived or worked on property belonging to another.

province—An administrative district of an empire or kingdom.

Renaissance—The era of new developments in European culture that began in Italy before 1400 C.E., inspired by European scholars' rediscovery of the civilizations of ancient Greece and Rome.

tribute—A payment from a weaker to a stronger power, usually under the threat of force.

500 C.E. Clovis, founder of the Frankish state, conquers most of France and Belgium.

700–1200 Europe has unusually mild weather. Agriculture spreads into the northern part of the continent.

768 Charlemagne comes to the Frankish throne, begins to build a European empire, and launches a revival of learning.

871–899 King Alfred the Great of England promotes unity among Anglo-Saxon states.

962 Otto I, king of Germany, is crowned emperor.

1050–1300 European politics, economy, and culture flourish during the High Middle Ages. The papacy takes on some characteristics of a monarchy.

1066 French nobleman William the Conqueror invades England and claims the throne.

1071 Seljuq Turks conquer the eastern parts of the Byzantine empire.

1095–1099 The Crusades begin when Pope Urban II sends crusaders to capture Jerusalem from the Muslims.

1180 King Philip of France liberates western France from English control and begins establishing a modern French state.

1187 Muslims retake Jerusalem.

1200 European cities and states see rise in long-distance trade.

1212 Christian forces regain Spain from Muslims.

1215 English nobles force King John to accept the Magna Carta, a document that limits royal power and makes kings subject to law.

1240 Mongols seize Kiev in southern Russia.

1272 King Edward I of England establishes parliament as a feudal court. Eventually it will become the center of English representative government.

1305 The papacy is moved from Rome to Avignon, France. The French dominate the papacy for almost a century.

1328 England tries to rule France.

1337–1453 France and England fight the Hundred Years' War.

1347 The Black Death appears for the first time in medieval Europe.

1358 Aristocrats crush a revolt, the Jacquerie, by French peasants.

1381 King Richard II puts down the English Peasants' Revolt.

Chronology

1453 Ottoman Turks capture Constantinople, bringing the Byzantine empire to an end.

1455–1485 England is torn by the War of the Roses, which ends when Henry VII founds the Tudor dynasty.

1492 Ferdinand of Aragon and Isabella of Castile, the joint rulers of Spain, drive Jews out of Spain and sponsor Christopher Columbus's voyage, which leads to the European discovery of the Americas.

Further Reading

Books

Corbishley, Mike. *The Middle Ages*. New York: Facts On File, 1990.

Corrick, James A. *The Late Middle Ages*. San Diego: Lucent Books, 1995.

Hanawalt, Barbara A. *The Middle Ages: An Illustrated History*. New York: Oxford University Press, 1998.

Hinds, Kathryn. Life in the Middle Ages (series). New York: Benchmark Books, 2001.

Howarth, Sarah. *Medieval People*. Brookfield, CT: Millbrook Press, 1992.

———. *Medieval Places*. Brookfield, CT: Millbrook Press, 1992.

Jordan, William C., ed. *The Middle Ages: An Encyclopedia for Students*. New York: Scribner and the American Council of Learned Societies, 1996. 4 volumes.

Langley, Andrew. *Medieval Life*. New York: Dorling Kindersley, 2000.

Oakes, Catherine. *Exploring the Past: The Middle Ages*. San Diego: Harcourt Brace Jovanovich, 1989.

WEB SITES

www.learner.org/exhibits/middleages
Aimed at students, this Middle Ages site is designed to answer the question, What was it really like to live in the Middle Ages? It has sections on feudal life, religion, the arts, homes, clothing, and other topics.

www.emuseum.mnsu.edu/history/middleages
Minnesota State University's site The Middle Ages explores the worlds of medieval knights, nuns, merchants, and peasants.

www.orb.rhodes.edu
The Online Reference Book for Medieval Studies, a site maintained by scholars, includes an encyclopedia, online textbooks, and collections of links to other sites as well as resources for nonspecialists.

www.eawc.evansville.edu/mepate.html
Medieval Europe, part of the University of Evansville's Exploring Ancient World Cultures site, offers essays on many topics as well as a time line of the Middle Ages, a quiz, and resources such as the text of the Magna Carta.

www.historyforkids.org/learn/medieval
The history department at Portland State University in Oregon operates History for Kids, a site devoted to introducing students to history. Their Middle Ages page covers Europe, Asia, and Africa before 1500 and includes many entries that can be searched either by region or by topic.

ABOUT THE AUTHOR

Rebecca Stefoff is the author of Marshall Cavendish's North American Historical Atlases series, the *Young Oxford Companion to Maps and Mapmaking,* and many other nonfiction books for children and young adults. You can find a list of her books at www.rebeccastefoff.com. History, geography, and maps are among her special interests. Stefoff has written about exploration in the Middle Ages in *Marco Polo and the Medieval Explorers* (Chelsea House, 1992) and *The Viking Explorers* (Chelsea House, 1993), and she also wrote many articles for *The Middle Ages: An Encyclopedia for Students* (Scribner and the American Council of Learned Societies, 1996). She makes her home in Portland, Oregon.

Index

Page numbers in **boldface** are illustrations.